I0883012

Table of Contents

Rourke Educational Media

A Division of Carson Dellosa Education

rourkeeducationalmedia.com

Can you find these words?

country

history

law

patriotism

Independence Hall

A symbol stands for an idea.

Independence Hall is in Philadelphia, Pennsylvania.

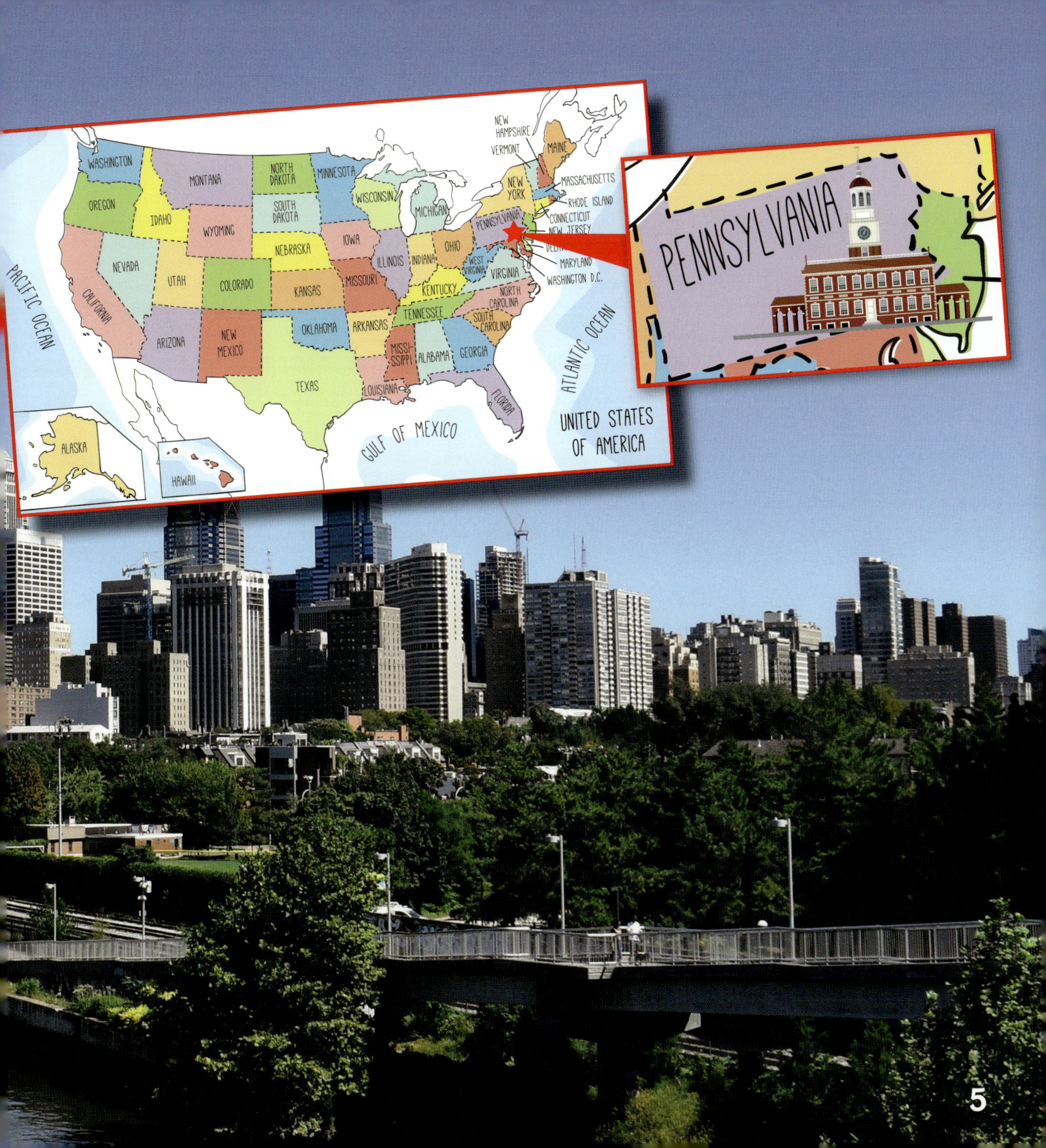
WASHINGTON
OREGON
CALIFORNIA
NEVADA
IDAHO
MONTANA
WYOMING
UTAH
ARIZONA
COLORADO
NEW MEXICO
NORTH DAKOTA
SOUTH DAKOTA
NEBRASKA
KANSAS
OKLAHOMA
TEXAS
MINNESOTA
IOWA
MISSOURI
ARKANSAS
LOUISIANA
WISCONSIN
ILLINOIS
MICHIGAN
INDIANA
OHIO
KENTUCKY
TENNESSEE
MISSI-SSIPPI
ALABAMA
GEORGIA
FLORIDA
SOUTH CAROLINA
NORTH CAROLINA
VIRGINIA
WEST VIRGINIA
PENNSYLVANIA
NEW YORK
NEW HAMPSHIRE
VERMONT
MAINE
MASSACHUSETTS
RHODE ISLAND
CONNECTICUT
NEW JERSEY
MARYLAND
WASHINGTON D.C.
ALASKA
HAWAII
PACIFIC OCEAN
ATLANTIC OCEAN
GULF OF MEXICO
UNITED STATES OF AMERICA
PENNSYLVANIA

It is a symbol of freedom.

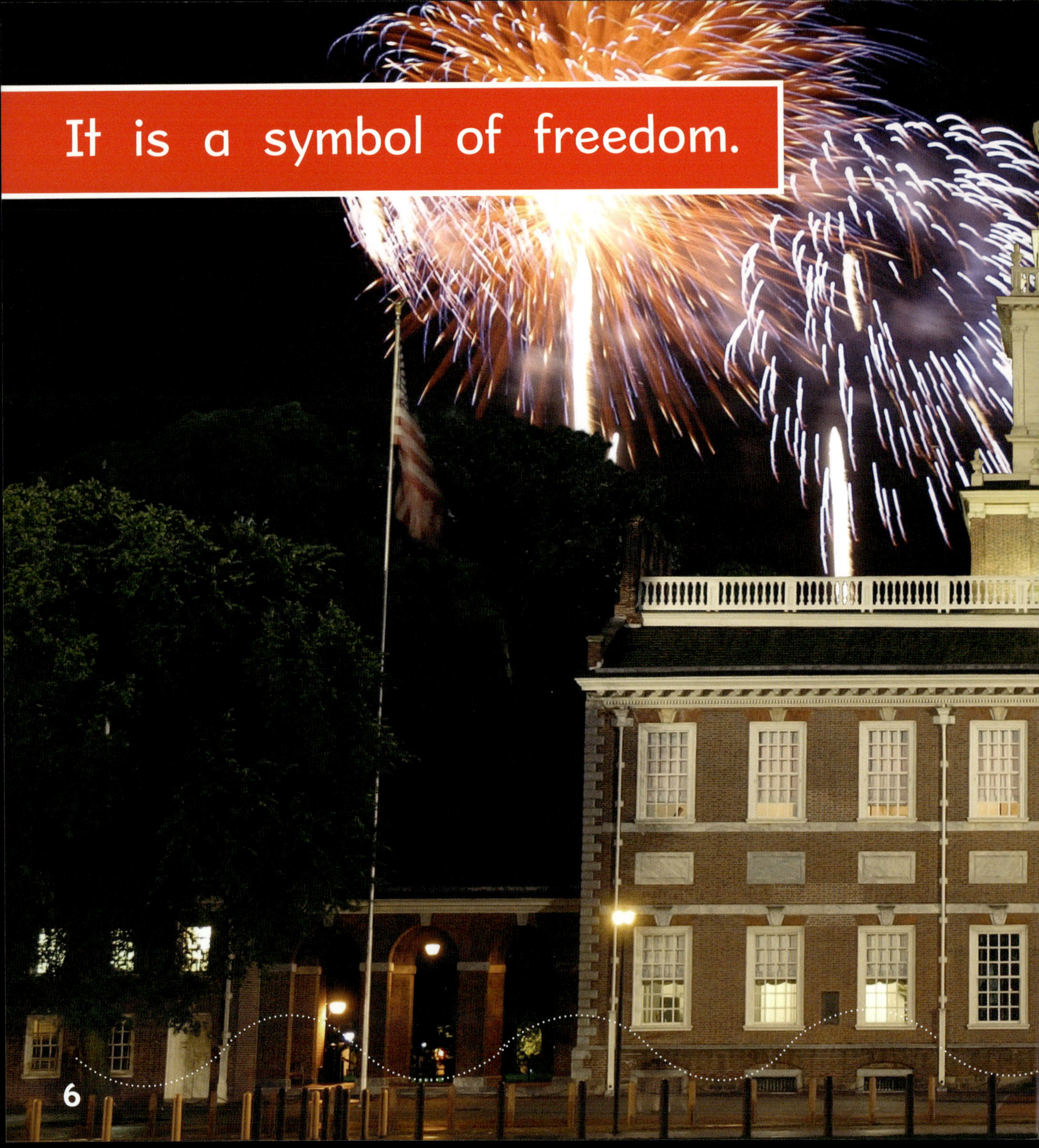

It is a symbol of **patriotism.**

The Declaration of Independence was signed here.

It says the United States is a free **country**.

The U.S. Constitution was signed here.

It is the top **law** in the country.

Many people visit Independence Hall.

They visit to learn about the country's **history**.

Did you find these words?

It says the United States is a free **country**.

They visit to learn about the country's **history**.

It is the top **law** in the country.

It is a symbol of **patriotism**.

Photo Glossary

country (KUHN-tree): A part of the world with its own territory and government.

history (HIS-tur-ee): Things that happened in the past.

law (law): A rule established and enforced by a government.

patriotism (PAY-tree-uh-tiz-um): Love and loyalty for one's country.

Index

About the Author

K.A. Robertson is a writer and editor who enjoys learning about the history of the United States. She likes to visit Independence Hall and the Liberty Bell in Philadelphia.

© 2020 Rourke Educational Media
All rights reserved. No part of this book may be reproduced or utilized in any form or by any means, electronic or mechanical including photocopying, recording, or by any information storage and retrieval system without permission in writing from the publisher.

www.rourkeeducationalmedia.com

PHOTO CREDITS: Cover: ©HaizhanZheng; Pg 2, 10,14, 15 ©oersin; Pg 2, 13, 14, 15 ©ggustin; Pg 2, 6, 14, 15 ©trekandshoot; Pg 2, 8, 14, 15 ©Carol M. Highsmith: Photographer, Library of Congress; Pg 3 ©Steve Debenport; Pg 4 ©curtrog

Edited by: Kim Thompson
Cover and interior design by: Kathy Walsh

Library of Congress PCN Data
Independence Hall / K.A. Robertson
(Visiting U.S. Symbols)
ISBN 978-1-73160-572-6 (hard cover)(alk. paper)
ISBN 978-1-73160-420-0 (soft cover)
ISBN 978-1-73160-621-1 (e-Book)
ISBN 978-1-73160-657-0 (ePub)
Library of Congress Control Number: 2018967351

Printed in the United States of America,
North Mankato, Minnesota